Symphonies of Life

Nagalakshmi Neeraja Paramatmuni

Copyright © 2024 Nagalakshmi Neeraja Paramatmuni

Made with ❤ on the Notion Press Platform

www.notionpress.com

I dedicate this book to everyone who entered my life and made a lasting impression, making me pen these poems.

CONTENTS

Contents

Foreword

Neeraja writes with a vibrant imagination. Each poem of hers is a doorway, a glimpse into the emotions where joy and sorrow, love and loss, hope and despair co-exist in a delicate dance. In this collection, may you discover reflections on your journey, moments of connection, and the poetic spirit's timeless beauty.

As we step into this realm of verse, let us surrender to the rhythms that speak to us in ways prose cannot. Within these lines, we find a sanctuary of words, a tapestry woven from the threads of human fervour. Welcome to a journey to a heart's terrain, where every poem is a step towards greater understanding and empathy. Each poem in this collection is a mirror, reflecting the myriad aspects of our inner world. Her poetry stands as a beacon illuminating our hearts.

Pavan Kumar Paramatmuni

Msc. Bio Sciences, MHA Hospital Administration

16th June 2024

About the Author

Nagalakshmi Neeraja is a person who enjoys the world of literature. She weaves her experiences and human emotions into poems. Since childhood, she had a keen interest in reading books or listening to stories. We as her parents kept nurturing her by encouraging her to read different books and tales. This early exposure to the charm of words set her on the path to explore and create her own imaginations and narrations.

She is currently residing in Mysore and doing her first year of higher secondary education. Neeraja discovered her ability to write poems when she was in the 9th grade while studying at Podar International School. Her English teacher and school counsellor have become the light and the path for the flow of her poetry. Her school counsellor assorted all her poems which emerged as a binded book to boost her confidence in her writing skills.

We have been quite supportive of her exploring new ideas and letting her imagination soar. We could observe the poetry power of hers can touch hearts and inspire others. Her sister is her first and best audience as she always gets the first look at her new poems.

Neeraja invites readers into nature's lap and sojourns awhile with the poems like a sunbeam's smile.

Pavan Kumar Paramatmuni

29th May 2024

Acknowledgments

I'm deeply indebted to my parents for their selfless love and support. I always knew that you believed in me and wanted the best for me. A simple thanks would surely fall short of everything you both have done for me. Please accept my deepest gratitude for trusting in me and my talent.

I want to express my gratefulness to my English teacher, Mr Matthew, and my compassionate school counsellor, Ms Anitha Blessie for consistently boosting my confidence and helping me realize my potential. I am deeply grateful for their unwavering support and guidance. Their encouragement and mentorship have been instrumental in transforming my self-confidence and helping me discover my true capabilities.

My heartfelt gratitude also to my paternal and maternal grandparents for their unconditional love towards my work of poetry.

I am grateful to acknowledge the invaluable support and encouragement of my friends and classmates, who served as my initial audience and provided valuable feedback.

I'm very thankful for Ms. Sujata Rajpal who also had a hand in the emergence of this book.

I've always been deeply inspired by the timeless poetry of Robert Frost. His ability to capture profound truths about life and human nature in his verses is something I often get inspired to achieve in my writing. One of his poems that has left a lasting impact on me is "The Road Not Taken," which produces deep emotion towards choice and destiny.

I hope the one who picks it enjoys this cruise over the sea of emotions!
Thank you.

Yours,
Nagalakshmi Neeraja Paramatmuni

Eyes as the Canvas

Eyes (25th January 2023)

Sometimes up, sometimes down,

of course, this side to that one.

That's how her kohl-filled eyes move!

Who knows, what she'd be searching for,

her anxious eyes are always restless.

I wonder how those eyes would look

when they've found what they want.

Insights from the author: This is a description of a pair of eyes filled with kohl that keep searching for something they are unaware of. I used to be quite close to her and have seen her eyes taking silent peeks and searching for something her eyes couldn't reach.

Those eyes (10th March 2023)

Though I'm too afraid of-

bugs, bees, flies, and snakes,

What scares me the most-

are those angry eyes.

I always try to escape,

yet somehow get caught!

Those reddish-yellow eyes-

stare me out of anger,

just like a panther-

staring at its prey!

Those scary eyes

are as sharp as a blade.

Those creepy eyes

are as blazy as a fire.

I wish I were invisible!

Insights from the author: This is a description of a pair of eyes that set fire in the viewer's hearts that they wish to be invisible to those eyes. I've never seen these eyes in calm and compassionate mode; in contrast, they keep growling in fury.

Few eyes (27th April 2023)

There are few eyes around,

that hunt and haunt me.

Those sights poke me

and make me feel insecure.

The whole world doesn't bother,

yet those few eyes do!

They leave me differentiated-

and discriminated among 'em.

It's just the work of-

few eyes among the rest.

Insights from the author: Actions speak louder than words. Eyes speak more than what a mouth does. Eyes curse more than what a mouth does. One would surely come across these kinds of eyes anywhere and anytime. But self-confidence and courage will always aid in giving them an eye of an eye!

Your Eyes (25ᵗʰ September 2023)

Millions of eyes around,

yet mine meet yours.

In this busy crowd

I just search for-

your twinkling eyes.

A moment's sight,

overflows with-

doubtful compassion.

You wanna speak,

but dunno how to.

I wanna speak;

Nah, I'm just fine

conversing the poem-

of love, with your eyes!

Insights from the author: There can be many languages without a scripture, and one of them is the language of eyes…The only prettiest languages ever spoken without mouth.

The Obsession (13ᵗʰ July 2023)

Once I fell into an obsession-

of drawing eyes.

Just couldn't stop the self-

from drawing 'em at all!

When found a pencil,

I gave life to many eyes.

Happy with the result,

I drew many, many more!

Many pages, tables and walls-

Got filled with eyes.

But all of 'em-

once got creepy!

I felt being stalked,

as they were almost everywhere!

All that started,

with one big obsession.

Insights from the author: Sometimes, obsession turns out to be scary! Here's an illusionary example. I got into this obsession once.

A Tangled Tale

My lost piece of heart (4th Feb 2023)

I was searching for my lost piece of heart,

not knowing that it's you.

You were just around me,

Yet I couldn't recognise you!

Now that you're gone,

I realize it's you!

I still live in your presence-

though you've left me.

Where are you?

I still won't give up.

I'll go on searching for you,

Even if I had to cross--

The seas, oceans, skies;

Just for you!

Insights from the author: When a person is around us, we often don't understand their importance. Once they're gone, we tend to miss them. Even if we keep searching for them or keep pleasing them, they'll be gone. Once gone, gone forever. Be grateful for the ones near you and care for you.

A broken friendship (10th February 2023)

Lemme capture you in my eyes,

Lemme captivate you in my mind,

Lemme charm you in my heart-

At least these last days of my life.

Be around my eyes, until I close 'em.

Your presence can heal-

my broken heart that beats for you!

Your presence can cure-

my ill-fated soul that shines for you!

Here I am, lying on my deathbed,

waiting to see you with my teary eyes!

Insights from the author: Two close friends once got separated in their childhood. Their ego was the cause. In their old age, when one of the friends gets bedridden, she thinks of her old friend and yearns to meet her for one last time before she dies. Ego kills relations. There is nothing wrong with compromising for the sake of friendship.

Those bunch of girls (28th February 2023)

Those bunch of girls,

who was nice to me,

why aren't they now?

They still speak sugary words,

but why do they have other-

intentions that I'm unaware of?

Their rude talks about me,

they speak behind me,

why did I trust them so long?

I'm a person of few words,

though aware, they ignore me!

I'm a left-out, sobbing behind.

They cry at my success,

laugh at my failure,

yet pretend to be a friend of mine!

Insights from the author: Everyone around acts. They have different intentions. They pretend to be a friend, a companion, a person to trust. Beware of the kind of people around. Never give personal information to everyone. One has to keep an individual space where no one can enter, even their closest pals.

Dearest Ego (3rd March 2023)

Time flies, Time flies, Time flies!

Closest friends became sworn enemies,

Small fights became big disputes,

They no longer talk with each other.

Both hope to end this fight.

Both want their friend back.

But one says, "Why me?"

And the other says, "Why me always?"

Their ego restricts them from apologizing.

When will this come to an end?

Will they be close friends again?

Insights from the author: Two friends get divided because of their egos. When both start to miss one another, they wait for each other to apologize. Will they be friends again?

A Faded Friend of Yours (7th December 2023)

You won't hold me,

You won't leave me.

You have me on your side-

as if I were an obligation.

I start to feel that-

we don't match anymore.

I start to think that-

we shouldn't patch anymore.

My importance got diluted,

many replaced my place,

I feel dislocated-

can you understand?

But I'm happy,

that you'll be happy-

even in my absence!

From: A faded friend of yours.

Insights from the author: Priorities change with time. And also, the importance we give to different people. Once you get habituated to receiving full priority from a person and suddenly they shift their priorities or start to neglect a bit, it starts to hurt. Here, in a friendship, a friend feels that she lost her friend to another one and became a burden to her. Since her friend consciously had to devote a separate time only for her, balancing with another person, this friend chose to isolate herself.

Broken Bond (2nd March 2024)

A warm smile, a promise given,

A warm smile, the promise broken.

Held a hand and gave the trust,

Left the hand and broke the trust.

Even a strong iron gets rusted,

Even a strong bond gets broken.

While counting their tears,

they forgot to count their-

Happy times together!

Insights from the author: Trust broken is a bond broken. But forgiveness is the greatest blessing one can give or receive. Before deciding to get rid of a relationship re-think about the happy times, the decision might change! The only word that hurts the most in this world in a friendship is 'goodbye'. One must try to avoid it, otherwise, they might remain in guilt.

What if they meet again? (24th April 2024)

What if they meet again?
Many unspoken truths rush in mind,
old memories take rewind.
Two poor souls crave-
for a hug,
to reunite their bond.
A flood of tears run down.
An urge to smile again,
laugh again, tease again,
cry again, TOGETHER.
But an insecure voice-
echoes, 'history repeats.'

Insights from the author: This friendship had got a halt due to insecurity of one of them and the friends swore to never speak being unaware of each other's thoughts. They start to miss their time together as the days go on. When they meet after many years, they recollect their memories and want to embrace one another. But the insecure friend who also wants her friend back gets stopped by her fear.

Rhythms of Life

A Lost Life (2ⁿᵈ February 2023)

There she goes on a trip,

to find her lost life.

Wandering here and there,

just to get a chance-

to live once again!

She swam through the clouds,

over the rivers and seas.

Hoping to find it one day.

Will she get her lost-

Life back again?

Insights from the author: An abandoned soul tries to find her life again. When she was alive, she never gave time for herself and now when she's dead, she wants it back. And so, she travels around the world to find it once more.

A knock (7th March 2023)

There lived an unhappy man,

waiting for a change in his life.

Then came a sudden knock;

he rushed to open, and-

What he received was the disappointment.

Another time, another knock,

he again rushed but received-

The usual disappointment.

Hence, he got fooled again.

And this happened thrice!

The unhappy man, then-

heard a huge knock again,

but he gave up and ignored it.

The knock was stopped soon,

And there was silence all around.

When he peeped out

to see who it was,

It was the opportunity that just left.

He regretted his act-

of giving up at the right moment.

Insights from the author: 'Disappointment' knocks on the door and this man gets fooled all the time mistaking it as 'Opportunity'. But when the 'Opportunity' itself comes and knocks his door, he can't make out the difference and hence loses his chance to re-mould his life. And so, it is advised not to give up at any point in time. One might never be able to see the opportunity hiding in the clothes of disappointment. Here, both 'Disappointment' and 'Opportunity' are humanized.

People use me! (3ʳᵈ April 2023)

People use me! People use me!

I'm a tissue and an issue for them.

Come to me in need, and go-

away once done, am I a god?

I'm a human, a living one.

Talk to me, people! I'm alive!

No-no-no! Not back of me,

Talk to me, with me!

Insights from the author: Most tend to talk behind the back. They use the innocents for their benefit and leave them once done; unaware of the grief the latter undergoes. The ones with lesser self-confidence tend to gossip as they can't face the person they're talking about. In my opinion, the world is selfish. People will take anything seriously only if it fulfils their selfish motives. And it's the same condition with God. Many remember God when they have any worries or problems and beg him to be relieved. When their life goes smoothly, they won't think about him at all!

Insecurity (8th September 2023)

Keeping myself covered,

wrapped with many jackets-

And scarves, I walk

past the streets.

To avoid awkwardness,

I put up my glasses,

hands in my pockets,

chin facing the ground.

Finally, dusk swept-

the sky all over.

Now I take off-

all the coverings,

Standing at the ledge,

all by myself.

Peace, peace, peace.

I finally have some peace.

The world is asleep,

and there's none to judge.

I can run around and-

scream till I'm whacked.

Being tired of bearing-

fake smiles,

I can finally be happy.

A real smile is now-

lit on my face!

Insights from the author: Dear introverts, do you relate?

Cloudy Sky (13th July 2023)

Look at the cloudy sky,

that has both white and black clouds.

White ones with the bright sun, and

Black ones with the pleasant rain.

I may take the sun's aid,

to dry up my tears.

But can always cry on,

in the rain later.

My mood's just like-

the cloudy sky!

Filled with clouds-

that take any chance,

to burst out!

Insights from the author: Weather keeps on changing
and so are moods.

The sweetest sorry (13th May 2023)

Amongst these egoistic,

ignorant, forceful sorrys,

Someone genuinely said-

a heartfelt sorry.

It was a reply to my-

rude, sharp taunt.

That kind, warm sorry-

made me feel guilty for my act.

Because it's the sweetest-

sorry I've ever heard!

Insights from the author: When we get habituated to receiving an insult or rude reply for taunting or humouring a person for their wrong doings, a sorry or an apology seems to make us regret and ponder upon our words. And that sorry seems to be the sweetest and the purest sorry ever heard.

If I were you (1ˢᵗ Feb 2023)

If I were you,

I can eat and sleep

and dance and sing.

I can go and have fun

and have no worries.

I'll have your money,

clothes, house, car-

And what not!

But if you were me,

bet you'd hang next moment!

Insights from the author: A criminal would say this to a rich man before robbing his identity to escape from law and justice.

YOURSELF (19 December 2023)

You must rely on yourself,

O human! There isn't-

a soul left to trust on.

Breathe for yourself,

Sustain for yourself.

They, the foolish,

will call you selfish.

But are they selfless?

They are hopeless.

Live for yourself.

Believe in yourself.

You are for YOURSELF

Insights from the author: Not everyone is selfless in their acts and talks. Relying on others is like living for others. No other person should be the reason why one is alive. One is born alone and will die alone.

Others who come in between just go away later. But the self remains forever.

A Word (22ⁿᵈ December 2023)

So there's a word,

Of what people never utter.

Rigid of heart, filled with ego.

Right or wrong, they never spell.

Yes, they're aware,

yet never say.

What do you think, it is?

Insights from the author: What do you think that word is? (Check the 1st letters of 1st 5 lines)

Curiosity (28ᵗʰ January 2024)

Sometimes I feel,

I shouldn't have known a few things.

'Cause the more I know, the more I think.

The more I think, the more I realize.

The more I realize, the weirder things become.

Things that were just fine before-

now became more complex.

People who were quite normal before-

now became more worse.

All because of my curiosity-

to know people deeply.

Insights from the author: Keeping everyone at a distance is always the best. When their true nature is found out, one can never unsee it or be able to treat them the way they've done before and regret to know about them.

Memories (28th February 2024)

Some things remind me-

of the moments I smiled,

of the moments I cried,

of the moments I enjoyed,

of the moments I don't-

want anymore.

If I keep, I weep.

If I throw, I woe.

These memories stab me,

crush me, and ask me:

'Why did everything change?'

Insights from the author: Memories hurt more than people! I realized that it's better to avoid keeping souvenirs in memory of the ones (almost everyone who comes across in one's life) who would just walk away one day.

Twinkle Twinkle Little Star (17th May 2024)

Twinkle twinkle little star,
How I wonder what you are!
And so, I came-
flying all the way,
In hope to see the
tiny, cute you.
But I stood there,
aghast, seeing the
huge, blazing you.
Why aren't you,
the little star
that you seemed from far?
Why do you-
look one,
but are something else?
I come back home,
dispirited, and-
looked above
to see you, the little star-
twinkling high up there!

Insights from the author: All glitters aren't gold. Whatever is seen isn't the same as what it is. There are high chances of salt mixed in sugar. This isn't about salt or sugar. This isn't about stars. …

The Spirit of the Divine

A letter from God (30th March 2023)

You must keep walking,

may it be day or night.

I shall be behind you,

sheltering and protecting.

Why would you stop-

and turn back to confirm?

Don't you have any-

faith or trust in me?

I am in you,

with you, for you,

beside you, behind you,

above you and beneath you!

You just have to realize me

and keep walking past the

happy and sad times of life.

believe me, have faith in me.

Insights from the author: If God speaks to the person who lost hope in life, this is what he would say.

A lady with a lamp (4th July 2023)

She's a lady with a lamp of joy.

She ignites the fire of happiness-

and removes the sadness and depression.

Her sweet smile gives warmth,

enough warmth to forget the grief.

She's a lady with a lamp of positivity.

She ignites the fire of confidence-

and removes the fear and anxiety.

Her convincing talks encourage

enough to do wonders.

Insights from the author: I devote this poem to the person who believed in me and rebuilt the confidence I felt I was losing. Dear mam, thank you so much! :)

O God! (24th November 2023)

From swinging on the park's swing,

I now swing in your name.

O God! You are the wind,

that makes my swing swing.

From dancing for some random beats

I now dance in your name

O God! You are the music,

that makes my mind happy.

From writing poems from people,

I now write about you.

O God! You are the ink

that pours my thoughts onto the paper.

Insights from the author: God is the creator of us and the ultimate guide. He is everything and everywhere. We are just the spark of the fire called 'Almighty'.

He is far away from the material world and is above everything. Understanding him is a very big task for any human being.

A Tale of Fated Enmity

Pair of Enemies (12ᵗʰ August 2023)

Eight directions around,

yet they are bound to meet.

Seconds of gaze,

filled with hate.

Smiles fade away,

when around each other.

Faces frown,

to show their arrogance.

Silent wars amongst 'em-

yet act like strangers.

What a pair of enemies!

Insights from the author: This pair of enemies seem to be fated to hate each other. Right from when they met, they kept on hating each other. Even though they fight soundless battles, they prefer to act like strangers as if they are unaware of each other.

Fall in hate (5th January 2024)

All I want, is to

fall in hate with you.

You are the first person,

I've ever fallen in hate with!

I hate you-

for your deeds,

I hate you-

for your looks,

You too are in hate-

with me,

and we must cherish this!

As we hate to love each other,

'cause we love to hate each other.

Insights from the author: This is when enemies hate each other and want to put it positively, they express that they've fallen in hate with one another.

Whispers of the Wild

Dewdrop (3rd October 2023)

I'm a dewdrop,

small yet cute

Dancing on the edge-

of a red button rose.

Look through the life

from the tip of me,

You'll find the real beauty.

If not here, then where?

The bright twinkle-

of mine, add it to your smile.

You'll find real joy.

If not here, then where?

Insights from the author: Finding joy in small things is an art. Next time you see a dewdrop, add it to your smile! :D

Fear (3rd November 2023)

Whenever I think of you,

I see you around me.

The sight of you,

my eyes go wide!

I hear you talk,

my heart thunders!

When you're near me,

I try all the chances-

to escape from you.

Sometimes you come alone,

else with your gang.

My fear makes me hate you.

Why are you everywhere?

O Bee, have I avenged you-

in my past life?

Insights from the author: HONEY-BEE. I love honey as much as I hate bees! I fear bees mainly for their sound rather than for their sting.

Shine (5ᵗʰ December 2023)

One starry night,

among all the stars-

twinkling in the sky,

a pair of pebble-like eyes-

were the only ones,

that was shining brightly-

behind the bush.

I wondered if-

it was a rain of gems.

But it was those stars,

that descended-

to borrow their shine.

Insights from the author: What do you think could be behind the bushes? Who's eyes do you think would shine brighter than the stars?

Flower (19th December 2023)

I'd be in gloom

until you bloom.

Once you open,

my frown gets broken.

That's the dawn,

Oh, come on!

It's rare to see-

a shy bud,

flutter with glee!

Insights from the author: Bud opening as a flower usually occurs early in the morning, and seeing it is almost rare for us. Ever seen a shy bud that hesitates to open and finally opens? Ever seen a shy person finally opening up and speaking? That's the same!

Chronicles of the Clock

The you, the yourself (14th August 2023)

Why do you cry upon that-

dead old man?

Get up, dig a grave and

bury him in.

There isn't any point in thinking

-bout him and waste your time.

Enjoy the you, the yourself!

Why do you ponder upon that-

unborn new child?

He'd surely be healthy,

wealthy and happy.

There isn't any point in thinking

-bout him and waste your time.

Enjoy the you, the yourself!

Insights from the author: If time talks, 'the old man' is the past, 'you' is the present, and the 'unborn new child' is the future.

Time (7ᵗʰ October 2023)

Time started to tick backwards

I was suddenly in the past,

reviewing all my memories-

both cringe and cherished ones!

I rejoiced the wonderful moments

once again with utmost joy-

and laughed at those

I cried once!

I ran through the entire-

life of mine in a flash.

Guess it's time, O God!

take me to you.

Insights from the author: It is said that when a person dies, for the next seven minutes the brain shows their entire life like a dream. Time never ticks back. But if it does to someone, their time is up!

Embracing Everything

My lost happiness (23rd February 2023)

People urged me to write happy poems,

So I thought of attempting one.

But I had to ponder on a few things,

What is real happiness?

Where to find real happiness?

Why did my happiness go missing?

Thus I decided to search for it!

I crossed many seas, oceans, hills-

Rivers, valleys and whatnot?

Yet couldn't find my lost happiness.

On the way back, I saw a small pond,

I saw my reflection when I peeped in.

A light smile lightened my face,

I've found it! I've found my lost happiness!

Insights from the poet: To be honest, I was urged to write happy poems because my initial audience felt that my poems were too depressing. And this is how it turned out to be!

An Untitled Beauty (15th January 2024)

The bright white crescent moon above,

I remember your wide grin.

The orangish-red shade of the sky,

I remember your blushed cheeks.

You ask for your eyes?

yes, the stars that pretend-

to twinkle like yours!

The cool breeze of the spring,

that's the way you twirl around.

They'll surely think-

this is a boast.

But little do they know,

that you deserve a boast!

Insights from the author: Everyone is beautiful, in their way. This is when a girl with low confidence about her looks talks to herself looking in the mirror, building up her confidence while unable to meet the standards of society.

Happy Anniversary! (15th April 2023)

I don't write much letters,

Yet thought to pen down one!

Could there be any other occasion,

As special as this one?

Could there be any other festive,

As important as this one?

Nope! A blind no!

Here's to another year-

Of being great together, like always!

Can you believe, it's been 17 years,

And here's many more to add on!

This is the day, years back,

Two worlds became one.

Will anyone resist to celebrate?

Insights from the author: This poem is for my parents on their 17th anniversary. After knowing my ability to write, I thought of writing one on them. After all, they are my everything!

Enchanted (22nd July 2023)

Lemme dance in the -

rain that makes your eyes sparkle.

Lemme sing in the

breeze that makes your cheeks blossom.

Lemme swim in the -

words that flow through your lips.

Another day, another chance,

just to appear in front of you!

I love this new and-

unusual feeling,

That makes my-

heart leap,

soul fly, and

mind crazy!

Insights from the author: I believe, being enchanted in this spell, anyone could get butterflies even in their most hidden imaginations, too! This is a small description of anyone under this spell.

A worthy sacrifice (20th August 2023)

There could be diamonds,

pearls, gems and many more!

But all I ask for is your shoulder-

that carries silent burdens,

to lean on, forever!

I left all my possessions-

behind, just to possess you.

Running all along those valleys-

Under this icy moonlight,

I stand before you, gazing at you!

You're the one, whom I gaze-

Without an eye's wink.

Insights from the author: A princess leaves her
power, possessions, luxuries and royal life behind to

enjoy a simple life with her beloved. I feel this is a worthy sacrifice. What do you think?

All March to the loo! (12th June 2024)

You might've seen parades-
on a national day or a festive day.
Ever seen it every day?
I've seen it, for
almost the whole-lot
I lived so far.

There's a building,
where its people-
parade in their leisure
All march in a line,
All march with a zeal,
All march to the loo!

Insights from the author: This is a fun poem. And the building mentioned here is the school.

My Initial Poems

The hope of my life (20th August 2022)

I had no shelter to protect myself

I had no shoulder to shed my tears

I had no mate to express my grief.

Then I met her, who became my new hope of life.

She said, "Don't worry, dear earthling,

I shall be a companion for your pure soul."

To stop my tears, she started to shed few.

She made everything dark and asked the rain to pour.

The rain equalled my tears and no soul could suspect.

I cried…cried and cried, till I got exhausted.

From up, she, the one who is limitless,

started laughing at my temporary grief.

Till now, my dear reader,

I bet you've guessed who she is!

Insights from the author: This is the first poem I've written for my English homework in Grade 9.

Beyond the Sky (September 2022)

Upon the heavens, a black barren infinity,

A quiet, calm, still area of oneness existed.

There's a space,

where everything is in it.

Started ahead of time

and spread beyond the time.

Having a ball of fire in the centre,

All planets orbit it making it supreme.

Somewhere in between we find a blue crystal,

on which the moon fills the night with its light.

The gown worn by the space,

is filled with countless twinkling stars.

It looks quite beautiful in the night sky

Where one can enjoy its beauty in solitude.

Deep.. deep.. In the dark,

are hidden.. the unspoken secrets.

The black magnets, the invisible moons,

last but not the least, the birth of space.

Insights from the author: I've written this for my school magazine because my English teacher urged me to try writing one as I already wrote one. He always wanted me to never give up on this skill.

The selfless help (15ᵗʰ January 2023)

I give you flowers – yet don't spare me

I give you fruits – yet kill me

I provide you medicines – yet destroy me

I provide you rain – yet uproot me

I stand like a barrier,

I remain like a warrior,

I could be your shelter.

Yet, O sinner, murder me for your greed!

Travel (14ᵗʰ January 2023)

Though unaware where the road'd lead to,

I still continue to travel by it-

At least I can trust the roads, unlike the humans.

Amongst could be rocks, slopes, fallen trees,

I still continue to travel by it-

At least I can trust the roads, unlike the humans.

There may be animals waiting to make me their meal,

I still continue to travel by it-

At least I can trust the roads, unlike the humans.

May the moon rise and night go blind,

Yet I continue to travel by it-

At least I can trust the roads, unlike the humans.

Skyscrapers (2015)

Are you thinking that 'SKYSCRAPERS'

grow tired?

Yes, they will grow tired.

Can anyone give

the skyscrapers one chair to sit?

Are you thinking that 'SKYSCRAPERS'

shiver at frosty nights?

Yes, they will shiver at the frosty nights.

Can anyone give

the skyscraper, a sweater or a jacket?

Are you thinking that 'SKYSCRAPERS'

feel lonely because they have grown so tall?

Yes, they will feel lonely.

Can anyone grow tall and be its friend?

Are you thinking that 'SKYSCRAPERS'

want to sleep?

Yes, they want to sleep and never get up at all.

Can anyone give a bed for them?

Everyone said yes!!!

Beverages (2014)

Beverages, beverages,

Mr. Coffee and Mrs. Tea

Miss Cola and Baby lemon juice!

Oh! We also have uncle water.

What a perfect Beverages family !!

www.ingramcontent.com/pod-product-compliance
Lightning Source LLC
Chambersburg PA
CBHW021119130726
47988CB00003B/1085